FLY FISHING TALES

FLY FISHING TALES

Literary Bait by Angling Authors

Photographs by Terry Heffernan

Watercolor Paintings by Winslow Homer

Marbled Papers by Wendy Addison

VIKING STUDIO BOOKS

VIKING STUDIO BOOKS
Published by the Penguin Group
Viking Penguin, a division of Penguin Books USA Inc.,
375 Hudson Street, New York 10014, U.S.A.
Penguin Books Ltd, 27 Wrights Lane, London W8 5TZ, England
Penguin Books Australia Ltd, Ringwood, Victoria, Australia
Penguin Books Canada Ltd, 10 Alcorn Avenue, Suite 300, Toronto, Ontario, Canada M4V 3B2
Penguin Books (N.Z.) Ltd, 182-190 Wairau Road, Auckland 10, New Zealand
Penguin Books Ltd, Registered Offices: Harmondsworth, Middlesex, England
First published in 1994 by Viking Penguin, a division of Penguin Books USA Inc.

1 3 5 7 9 10 8 6 4 2

Grateful acknowledgment is made for permission to reprint the following copyrighted works:
"Fishing Wild" by Ted Williams from *Sports Afield* magazine, May 1976. Copyright © 1976 by The Hearst Corporation.
All rights reserved. By permission of the publisher and the author.
"Big Secret Trout" from *Trout Madness* by Robert Traver. Copyright © 1960 by Robert Traver.
Reprinted by permission Mrs. John D. Voelker.
"Clyde: The Metamorphosis" from *Confessions of a Fly Fishing Addict* by Nick Lyons. Copyright © 1989 by Nick Lyons. Reprinted by
permission of Simon & Schuster, Inc.
"Skelton's Party" from *Ninety-Two in the Shade* by Thomas McGuane. Copyright © 1973 by Thomas McGuane.
Reprinted by permission of Farrar, Straus & Giroux, Inc.
"Fishing Presidents and Candidates" from *Fishing for Fun* by Herbert Hoover. Copyright © 1963 by Herbert Hoover.
Reprinted by permission of Random House, Inc.
"The Best Rainbow Trout Fishing" from *Ernest Hemingway, Dateline: Toronto* by Ernest Hemingway. Copyright © 1985 by Mary
Hemingway, John Hemingway, Patrick Hemingway, and Gregory Hemingway. Reprinted by permission of
Charles Scribner's Sons, an imprint of Macmillan Publishing Company.
"The Line of Light" from *The River Why* by David James Duncan. Copyright © 1983 by David James Duncan.
Reprinted by permission of Sierra Club Books.

Credits for Winslow Homer paintings:
"Leaping Trout" (1889) and "Ouananiche Fishing, Lake St. John, Province of Quebec" (1897). Warren Collection,
courtesy of Museum of Fine Arts, Boston, Massachusetts.
"The Mink Pond" (1891). The Fogg Art Museum, Harvard University Art Museums, Cambridge, Massachusetts.

ISBN 0-670-85343-7
CIP data available.
Printed in Singapore

CONTENTS

ILLUSTRATIONS

DISTANT TOUCH

The Kanektok River slides out of low hills into the Kuskokwim delta on Alaska's Bering Sea littoral. The Yupik Eskimos in late June encamp along its alder-lined margins and set nets and wait for the salmon to return to spawn. The fish have always come. The Eskimos do not fish for fun; salmon have been their survival food for millennia. The salmon are retrieved from the nets anchored in the river, gutted, and hung in rows of red carcasses on wooden drying racks by the Eskimos' camps along the river.

In the late seventies white sport fishermen began to explore the river. They caught many salmon and rainbow trout.

And, strangely, they did not kill the fish. They released them to return to the river. The outside "modern" world, which had arrived at the Yupiks' doorstep in the shape of Russian fur traders several centuries before, was suddenly interested in something new — fishing for fun. And many of the fishermen were even stranger than the rest: they fished with flies instead of lures. And they were willing to pay princely sums to do it.

The two alien cultures, after centuries of exploitation by the one and severe confusion of the other, eyed each other with suspicion. On the river the sport fishermen motored upriver to their camps. When they

JOHN RANDOLPH

passed the Eskimo families gutting salmon on the gravel shingles, they would often wave tentatively. The waves would not be returned.

Eskimos had been heard to say that catching and releasing fish was immoral. Only fishing for food and survival was correct. It was as if something primal had been offended by the way the whites enjoyed themselves with the fish. Even before I got to the fishing camps, I felt a little uneasy. I had come in the summer of 1991 to recover something in myself. I feared that it might not be retrievable if I was watched by judgmental eyes. There had been enough of that back in the Lower 48.

What I sought on the river was a sense of distant touch, the inner relaxation in the soul that comes from a physical and spiritual encounter with a special wild creature — the kind of encounter that David James Duncan describes in his short story at the end of this book. It was important that the creature be a fish whose life cycle was epic and terminal. Only the Pacific salmon — and specifically the king — would serve. The king, you see, is the largest of all the salmon, reaching as much as 100 pounds, and by far the strongest. I hoped to catch a very large one before it reached the spawning beds, where its eyes would glaze with the supreme concentration of waning energy in its final renewal-of-life act before death. It was important to release the fish alive.

On the third day of fishing, from dawn until the Arctic summer sunset at 11 P.M., the fish I sought appeared as a russet-green shape in a run called the Fifteen Minute Hole. As I waded toward the torpedo shape, I planned the presentation of the fly — upstream

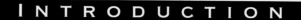

to a point above the fish so that the streamer would sink to tick bottom just in front of the salmon's nose.

It took fifteen minutes of casting to get the fly down just right. I could feel it tick gravel at just the right spot. The fish clearly moved its head and the line stopped momentarily. I lifted and felt the solid throb of life. The huge king surged down and across the river and jumped in an attempt — once, then twice — to free the hook. Then it turned downriver toward the sea and began what would become an epic journey of three miles of river and an hour and a half of struggle.

When I finally held the great fish, its strength vibrated, despite the jumping and thrashing fight. Its eye was a clear cobalt; its stare was as fixed and fierce as that of an eagle. Its flanks were firm and its back a chord of muscled energy so electric that when touched the life force in it caused my arm to tingle. At that moment a tight cold ball deep within me warmed. It melted as I revived the salmon. The fish suddenly shot from my hands, away from the gravel bar and into the river.

I fished then with the intensity of a true hunter. There would be no twinge of guilt in my reenactments. I had met and touched the pure wild thing on its way to a final act, the life giver passing a baton of genes. In that brief meeting I had taken something from the fish. What I had received renewed me.

The writers in this anthology seek and find the same renewals I found there on the Kanektok.

FISHING WILD

Down in Maine, when they say "fly-fishing only" they mean fishing only the way a gentleman would fish, for fish only a gentleman would fish for. In other words, casting dry flies to trout or salmon and — if one must — wets, too, though the latter act is regarded as questionable at best, somewhat akin to picking up chicken wings with one's fingers.

If you troll a fly on fly-fishing-only water or even drag a sloppy backcast with the wind, there is always the possibility that a Maine warden will pop out at you from the bank cover. Hidden, they will watch you for hours the way eagles watch dead deer. For them there is no such thing as a "secret" pond, and they think nothing of hoofing five miles through thick woods.

Most of the East's truly great brook trout water is in Maine, and most of that is restricted to fly-fishing. There are those who regard fly-fishing-only regulations as patently un-American. It is easy and, I confess, rather fun to infuriate them with a charade of country-club snobbery. They wax wild and irrational, spewing Jeffersonian democracy. Most of them are gentle, beautifully innocent souls, and I am burdened with the shame of having baited them. Still, I can't help noticing them among the opening-day hoard

TED WILLIAMS

that waves stubby, stout-lined spinning rods and vies gull-like for domestic trout that the state doles out each spring like so many haddock heads. In no way do I mean to assert that such carnivalizing is wrong, but in no way should it be confused with trout fishing.

Ironically, few vociferous critics of fly-fishing-only have ever fly-fished themselves, or at least experienced fly-fishing as an art form. Few have ever navigated through the big woods to fish a real trout pond for real trout. And yet they rail against the state for pandering to "blue-blooded elitists," charging that the ponds are restricted because they are great, never considering the possibility, and indeed the fact, that they are great because they are restricted. They have difficulty in understanding, for instance, that flies simply do not kill trout and that it serves little purpose to release fish whose gullets or gills have recently been festooned with big, thick-wired hooks. Nor do they easily understand that ten fly-fishermen can work an evening rise together (if they have to) and that one spincaster can slosh along, launch a door hinge into the middle of things and send every trout in the pool screaming for cover. Too much of any good thing is bad. This is a fundamental law of the cosmos that may be applied to everything from waffles to personal liberty.

I began fly-fishing Maine trout as an errant freshman at Colby College in Waterville. When the willows began to yellow along Johnson Pond, we would shake the leaders from our dusty books and jeep northward to begin what I considered then and consider now to be the most valuable part of our education.

We had our favorite spots which we renamed as a precaution against careless barroom

conversation. There was "Split-Mountain Sump," "Boty" and, most treasured of all, "Secret Pond" within a morning's walk of the fabled St. John River. The best was always "secret" something. The finest grouse covert we ever found, a popple-laced tote road teeming with "pat'ridges," was known around Waterville (after we'd graduated of course) as "Secret Road." The name stuck until 1973 when the pulpmen thoughtfully moonscaped it.

We discovered Secret Pond the same way we discovered all our ponds — scowling over a topo late into the night checking ponds in steeply contoured, roadless watersheds against the list of fly-fishing-only ponds in the booklet that comes with your fishing license.

I cannot, of course, tell you the real names of any of the ponds we fished or fish. Not only would it be a nefarious offense against common angling decency, it would ruin your fun. Choosing a pond for yourself, finding your way into it and emerging full-creeled from the wilderness is all part of the magic that makes Downeast fly-fishing the poignant and intensely personal experience it is. Though my fishing accomplices will furiously deny it, the hard truth is that the trouting in our ponds was, and is, not a whit better than the trouting in most of Maine's 153 fly-fishing-only ponds. All have healthy populations of squaretails that, thanks to flies-only and remote settings, are not significantly affected by fishing pressure. On many, one can fish a whole season without seeing a dozen anglers.

Finding your own pond in Maine is like finding your own woman. Basically, they're all put together the same way, but you become attached to a particular one for her individual topography. After you have lived with a few (ponds that is) you will be able to identify subtle variations in the trout from each. Split-Mountain Sump's, as I recall, were plump and black, Boty's sleek and silvery, Secret Pond's very orange. Obviously, some differences reflect the physiological response of the individual to his environment, but others reflect the evolutionary response of a population. Wisely, Maine has never stocked any of her truly wilderness trout ponds. To do so could bring about destruction of a pond's genetic identity established over millennia. The trout inhabiting such ponds are uniquely suited to their particular environments as are no other trout on earth.

I remember vividly the first day I fished Secret Pond. I was with my old roommate, Bob Daviau, a lifelong resident of Waterville who believes in his heart that Maine is supported by giant tortoises and that her borders fall away into primal chaos. Bob had pilfered the pond from his father, Jerome, one of Maine's renowned fly-fishermen, an attorney and author of *Maine's Lifeblood* — an expose of the paper industry's hog-greedy assault on the state's rivers and watersheds and of the spineless politicians who have permitted it.

Bob and I packed our gear late into the crisp June night, then left without having slept. All the way up, he was swearing me to secrecy. Mostly, he was afraid of his father's finding out he had betrayed the pond to an out-of-stater. An in-stater would have been bad enough — grounds for disownment at the least — but an *out-of-stater*. It was unspeakably heinous. I was not to let on I had even fished with Bob. And *never*, under any circumstances, was I *ever* to tell *anyone*, even my wife, should I ever have one, the location of Secret Pond.

In the predawn, with northern lights still flickering ahead of us, we pulled onto a rough logging road and jounced twenty miles into black wilderness. A woodland jumping mouse bounced down the headlight beam like a miniature kangaroo. Wood thrushes fluttered up like moths. We saw the glowing eyes and frozen silhouettes of deer, and once a young moose crossed casually in front of us.

We hid the jeep behind dripping spruces, brilliant in the breaking dawn. For long seconds, we inhaled the heady fragrance of balsam and wet, fresh earth, then walked backward into the woods, sweeping away our spoor with spruce bows. After the first blowdown, we turned and settled down to a fast-clipped hike over two miles of ancient, ingrown tote road, up one mountain, down another and, finally, by compass through thick trailless puckerbush.

We panted over a ridge, and there it was, rippling here and there in the morning wind, but mostly dark green and glassy in the shadow of protecting conifers.

I took a deep, steadying breath and started rigging my fly rod. Then we walked quickly to the rafts — two ponderous affairs with precarious birch-limb seats and long poles of black spruce.

Rafts are a tradition on Maine's fly-fishing-only ponds. They last about eight years, then someone makes another pair. Secret Pond has probably a dozen devotees who know each other only vaguely but who are strangely close in a common love for the pond and a knowledge that they are among the very, very few who have come to understand the meaning of the Maine woods. When someone builds a raft, it goes without saying that it belongs to everybody. Usually, there are two just in case there's someone in ahead of you, though it rarely happens.

Bob set me up near some dry-ki in the spring hole, and, with the kind of certainty that makes Downeasters impossible to argue with, announced that we'd really be wasting our time until 9 a.m. when "she turns on like an alarm clock." With that he poled for the big pond, back through the shallow thoroughfare whose mud bottom was a mass of moose prints, some still cloudy.

I started fishing grasshoppers on top. ("Anybody who don't go into them woods with a pocketful of grasshoppers ain't been fly-fishin' in Maine," I was once informed.) For half an hour, I bounced them off the dry-ki and skittered them around, so that they sent inviting little circles radiating out to blend into the moss-lined banks. Ravens croaked. After a long squint skyward I spotted them, two pencil dots on unbroken blue. Over on the big pond I could see a pair of loons and, in a cove near the beaver house, Daviau casting rhythmically. I had to admit that he handled a fly rod well. His backcasts were long and slow and powerful. They never even nicked the surface.

Without changing the 6X leader, I tied on a little Mickey Finn. On the third cast, a big

7

squaretail floated up through ten feet of transparent spring water, sliced the surface like a shark and sucked in the fly a rod-length from the raft. I struck, and he bored deep.

The winter had been long, and I rejoiced in this strange rite of spring — the sight and the feel of an arching rod, the tip dancing to the surface and below, and the yellow line slipping irresistibly down until it faded into dark refractions. I could feel heat between my thumb and forefinger, then the lump of the backing splice. I turned him with the splice halfway through the guides, marveling at his strength. At last I could see him spinning slow figure eights under the raft with two lesser trout attending on either flank like pilotfish. A minute later, I was gliding him into the wooden landing net. A gaudy cock fish, bass-fat and long as my forearm. I looked at my watch. It was 9 a.m.

The trout came fast for the rest of the morning, smaller than the first but all bright and in superb condition. Once, during that magic first day when I lay on the raft, viewing the bottom through cupped hands, feeling my belly tighten as the water between the logs soaked into my shirt, I saw something I have never seen before or since. A school of brook trout, perhaps 100, from a few ounces to several pounds, flowing along in close formation halfway between the surface and the bottom.

By noon, we had killed all the trout we could use and had released many more. There had even been a brief hatch of midges, and we had had a few minutes of fast action on top with No. 18 Black Gnats. For once we were sated.

We poled to shore and anchored the rafts by pushing the poles between the logs and

into the mud bottom. We hung on them so that they sunk in another foot, then swung ourselves onto the bank.

In a spruce-needled clearing, we munched sandwiches and sucked water from an icy brooklet black with trout fry, just touching the surface with our lips so as not to disturb the bottom silt.

Northern Maine is among America's last big tracts of wild land. It exists in its present form not because its residents differ significantly from other Americans in their feelings toward the land, but simply because they are few in number. In Maine, as elsewhere in the U.S., rivers, lakes and forests are just commodities to be disposed of whenever the economic whims of special interests dictate.

If the Army Corps of Engineers gets its way, 90,000 acres of Maine wilderness, including the upper St. John River — one of the nation's last blue-ribbon brook trout streams — and its network of trout-filled tributaries will be drowned. Capitalizing on the hysteria brought on by the contrived gasoline shortage, the artful Engineers managed to wangle the support of many otherwise environmentally responsible legislators for this decade-old boondoggle, the annual scuttling of which had become a House tradition.

Actually, the two dams at Dickey and Lincoln, which would cost us working folk at least $1 billion, could not even provide a pathetic one percent of New England's needs.

Residents of the village of Fort Kent, which nestles delinquently into the St. John flood plain just north of Eagle Lake, are eager for their little share of the federal pork the project is supposed to pump into Maine. They maintain that the dams are necessary to protect them from spring floods, though the Corps used to say all they needed was a $500,000 dike. It would be far cheaper for us to allow the river to reclaim its ancient flood plain and buy each villager a San Clemente-style mansion in the state of his choice.

Massachusetts Congressman Silvio C. Conte, who led two unsuccessful fights to kill appropriations for preconstruction planning, calls regionalism the biggest problem he has faced in educating the public to the real costs of the Dickey-Lincoln dams.

"Many residents of Maine think the dams are going to be a cure-all for their problems," he says. "'Who are you from Massachusetts coming up here to tell us what to do with our river?' They say. What these people don't realize is it's not just their river; it belongs to the whole country. It's yours and mine, and once it's gone, it's gone forever."

According to former Massachusetts Fish and Game Director James M. Shepard, this is what the Dickey-Lincoln dams will cost America: "90,000 acres of fabulously productive wildlife habitat supporting bald eagles, moose, an estimated 2200 deer (enough to provide 30,000 hunter days per season), black bear, ruffed grouse, woodcock, thousands upon thousands of woodland birds (especially warblers); 17,600 acres of top-quality deer yards vital to deer miles away from the project area, 2800 acres of prime waterfowl breeding ground which unleashes on the Atlantic Flyway a steady stream of blacks, woodies, blue-winged teal and ringnecks; about 50 miles of super brookie fishing on the Big and Little Black rivers and many miles of smaller but equally productive feeder streams, about 57 miles of upper St. John which now offers wild trouting and canoeing at its absolute best; the natural beauty and wilderness value shattered by 150 miles of new power lines; much of beautiful Deboulie Mountain with its 24 pristine trout ponds. (The mountain will be carved up for fill. To give you an idea of how much will be needed, the dam at Dickey will be 1¾ miles long, 300 feet high and substantially bigger than Egypt's infamous Aswan Dam.) Finally, a timber resource yielding $666,000 a year will be drowned, and 30,000 acres of ugly 'bathtub ring' intermittently exposed as the reservoir fluctuates."

Secret Pond and the vast wilderness that embraces it may die with the St. John. But one thing Congress and the Corps cannot take from me is the memory of that first day with Bob Daviau — how we caught orange, porcelain-finned brookies until our wrists ached. How we cleaned them by the beaver-blocked outlet and packed them away in corn snow and sphagnum moss. How we lay on our backs, catnapping and listening to the warblers rustling through the spruce trees. And how we trudged out in the late afternoon sun with our jackets tied round our waists, spitting blackflies and saying nothing because Secret Pond and the sacred Maine woods had said it all.

Big Secret Trout

No misanthropist, I must nevertheless confess that I like and frequently prefer to fish alone. Of course in a sense all dedicated fishermen must fish alone; the pursuit is essentially  a solitary one; but sometimes I not only like to fish out of actual sight and sound of my fellow addicts, but alone too in the relaxing sense that I need not consider the convenience or foibles or state of hangover of my companions, nor subconsciously compete with them (smarting just a little over their success or gloating just a little over mine), nor, more selfishly, feel any guilty compulsion to smile falsely and yield them a favorite piece of water.

There is a certain remote stretch of river on the Middle Escanaba that I love to fish by myself; the place seems made of wonder and solitude. This enchanted stretch lies near an old deer-hunting camp of my father's. A cold feeder stream — "The Spawnshop," my father called it — runs through the ancient beaver meadows below the camp. After much gravelly winding and circling and gurgling over tiny beaver dams the creek gaily joins the big river a mile or so east of the camp. Not unnaturally, in warm weather this junction is a favorite convention spot for brook trout.

One may drive to the camp in an old car or

ROBERT TRAVER

a jeep but, after that, elementary democracy sets in; all fishermen alike must walk down to the big river — *even* the arrogant new jeepocracy. Since my father died the old ridge trail has become overgrown and faint and wonderfully clogged with windfalls. I leave it that way. Between us the deer and I manage to keep it from disappearing altogether. Since this trail is by far the easiest and closest approach to my secret spot, needless to say few, secretive, and great of heart are the fishermen I ever take over it.

I like to park my old fish car by the camp perhaps an hour or so before sundown. Generally I enter the neglected old camp to look around and, over a devotional beer, sit and brood a little over the dear dead days of yesteryear, or perhaps more morosely review the progressive decay of calendar art collected there during forty-odd years. And always I am amazed that the scampering field mice haven't carried the musty old place away, calendars and all.... Traveling light, I pack my waders and fishing gear — with perhaps a can or two of beer to stave off pellagra — and set off. I craftily avoid using the old trail at first (thus leaving no clue), charging instead into the thickest woods, using my rod case as a wand to part the nodding ferns for hidden windfalls. Then veering right and picking up the trail, I am at last on the way to the fabulous spot where my father and I used to derrick out so many trout when I was a boy.

Padding swiftly along the old trail — over windfalls, under others — I sometimes recapture the fantasies of my boyhood: once again, perhaps, I am a lithe young Indian brave — the seventh son of Chief Booze-in-the-Face, a modest lad who can wheel and

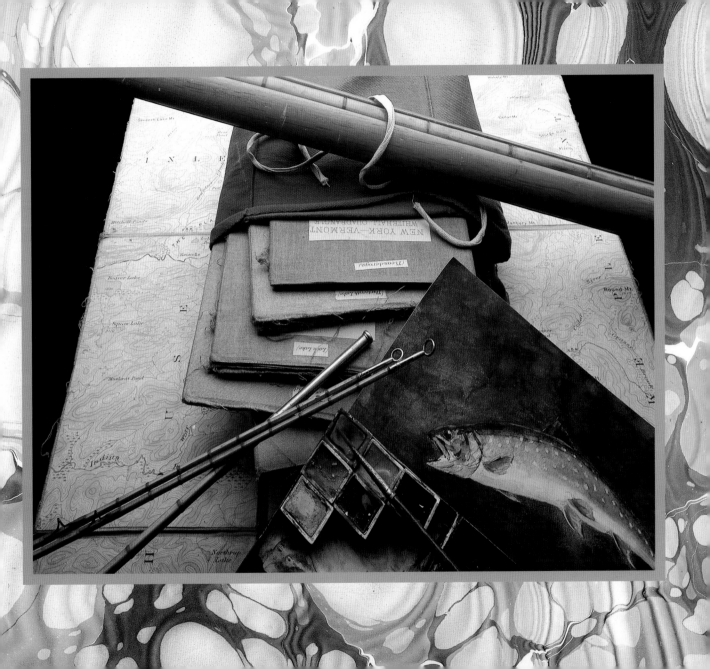

shoot the eye out of a woodchuck at seventy paces — not bound riverward to capture a great copper-hued trout for a demure copper-hued maiden; or again, and more sensibly, I am returning from the river simply to capture the copper-hued maiden herself. But copper fish or Indian maid, there is fantasy in the air; the earth is young again; all remains unchanged: there is still the occasional porcupine waddling away, bristling and ridiculous; still the startling whir of a partridge; still the sudden blowing and thumping retreat of a surprised deer. I pause and listen stealthily. The distant blowing grows fainter and fainter, "*whew*" and again "*whew*," like wind grieving in the pines.

By and by the middle-aged fisherman, still gripped by his fantasies, reaches the outlet of the creek into the main river. Hm . . . no fish are rising. He stoops to stash a spare can of beer in the icy gravel, scattering the little troutlings. Then, red-faced and panting, he lurches up river through the brambles to the old deer crossing at the gravel ford. Another unseen deer blows and stamps — this time across the river. "*Whew*," the fisherman answers, mopping his forehead on his sleeve, easing off the packsack, squatting there batting mosquitoes and sipping his beer and watching the endless marvel of the unwinding river. The sun is low, most of the water is wrapped in shadow, a pregnant stillness prevails. Lo, the smaller fish are beginning to rise. Ah, there's a good one working! Still watching, he gropes in the bunch grass for his rod case. All fantasies are now forgotten.

Just above his shallow gravel ford there is a wide, slick, still-running and hopelessly unwadable expanse of deep water — a small lake within the river. I have never seen a spot quite like it. On my side of this pool there is a steep-sloping sandy bank surmounted by a jungle of tag alders. On the far opposite bank there is an abrupt, rocky, root-lined ledge lined with clumps of out-curving birches, rising so tall, their quivering small leaves glittering in the dying sun like a million tinkling tambourines. But another good fish rises, so to hell with the tambourines. For in this mysterious pool dwell some of the biggest brown trout I know. This is my secret spot. Fiendishly evasive, these trout are not only hard to catch but, because of their habitat, equally hard to fish. The fisherman's trouble is double.

A boat or canoe invariably invokes mutiny and puts them down — at least any vessel captained by me. My most extravagant power casts from the ford below usually do the same or else fall short, though not always. The tall fly-catching tag alders on my side discourage any normal bank approach consistent with retaining one's sanity. (Hacking down the tag alders would not only be a chore, but would at once spoil the natural beauty of the place and erect a billboard proclaiming: BIG TROUT RESIDE HERE!) Across the way the steep rocky bank and the clusters of birches and tangled small stuff make it impossible properly to present a fly or to handle a decent trout if one could. The place is a fisherman's challenge and a fisherman's dream: lovely, enchanted, and endlessly tantalizing. I love it.

Across from me, closer to the other side and nicely out of range, there is a slow whirl-around of silky black water, endlessly revolving. Nearly everything floating into the pool —

including most natural flies — takes at least one free ride around this last merry-go-round. For many insects it is frequently the last ride, for it is here that the fat tribal chieftains among the brown trout foregather at dusk to roll and cavort. Many a happy hour I spent fruitlessly stalking these wise old trout. The elements willing, occasionally I even outwit one. Once last summer I outwitted two — all in the same ecstatic evening. Only now can I venture coherently to speak of it.

I had stashed my beer in the creek mouth as usual and had puffed my way through the tangle up to the deep pool. There they were feeding in the merry-go-round, *both* of them, working as only big trout can work — swiftly, silently, accurately — making genteel little pneumatic sounds, like a pair of rival dowagers sipping their cups of tea. I commanded myself to sit down and open my shaking can of beer. Above and below the pool as far as I could see the smaller brook trout were flashily feeding, but tonight the entire pool belonged to these two quietly ravenous pirates. "Slp, slp" continued the pair as I sat there ruefully wondering what a Hewitt or LaBranche or Bergman would do.

"They'd probably rig up and go fishin'," at length I sensibly told myself in an awed stage whisper. So I arose and with furious nonchalance rigged up, slowly, carefully, ignoring the trout as though time were a dime and there were no fish rising in the whole river, dressing the line just so, scrubbing out the fine twelve-foot leader with my bar of mechanic's soap. I even managed to whistle a tuneless obbligato to the steady "Slp, slp, slp...."

And now the fly. I hadn't the faintest idea what fly to use as it was too shadowy and too far away to even guess what they were taking. Suddenly I had *the* idea: I had just visited the parlor of Peterson, one of my favorite fly tiers, and had persuaded him to tie up a dozen exquisitely small palmer-tied creations on stiff gray hackle. I had got them for buoyancy to roll-cast on a certain difficult wooded pond. Why not try one here? Yet how on earth would I present it?

Most fishermen, including this one, cling to their pet stupidities as they would to a battered briar or an old jacket; and their dogged persistence in wrong methods and general wrongheadedness finally wins them a sort of grudging admiration, if not many trout. Ordinarily I would have put these fish down, using my usual approach, in about two casts of a squirrel's tail. Perhaps the sheer hopelessness of the situation gave me the wit to solve it. Next time I'll doubtless try to cast an anvil out to stun them. "The *only* controlled cast I can possibly make here," I muttered, hoarse with inspiration, "is a *roll* cast . . . yes — it's that or nothing, Johnny me bye." If it is in such hours that greatness is born, then this was my finest hour.

Anyone who has ever tried successfully to roll-cast a dry fly under any circumstances, let alone cross-stream in a wide river with conflicting currents and before two big dining trout, knows that baby sitting for colicky triplets is much easier. For those who know not the roll cast, I shall simply say that it is a heaven-born cast made as though throwing an overhand half-hitch with a rope tied to a stick, no back cast being involved. But a roll cast would pull my fly under; a decent back cast was impossible; yet I had to present a floating fly. *That* was my little problem.

"Slp, slp, slp," went the trout, oblivious to the turmoil within me.

Standing on the dry bank in my moccasins I calmly stripped out line and kept rolling it upstream and inshore — so as not to disturb my quarry — until I figured my fly was out perhaps ten feet more than the distance between me and the steadily feeding trout. And that was plenty far. On each test cast the noble little gray hackle quickly appeared and rode beautifully. "God bless Peterson," I murmured. Then I began boldly to arc the cast out into the main river, gauging for distance, and then — suddenly — I drew in my breath and drew up my slack and rolled out the fatal business cast. *This was it*. The fly lit not fifteen feet upstream from the top fish — right in the down whirl of the merry-go-round. The little gray hackle bobbed up, circled a trifle uncertainly and then began slowly to float downstream like a little major. The fish gods had smiled. Exultant, I mentally reordered three dozen precious little gray hackles. Twelve feet, ten feet, eight . . . holding my breath, I also offered up a tiny prayer to the roll cast. "Slp, slp..." The count-down continued — five feet, two feet, one foot, "slp" — and he was on.

Like many big browns, this one made one gorgeous dripping leap and bore down in a power dive, way deep, dogging this way and that like a bulldog shaking a terrier. Keeping light pressure, I coaxed rather than forced him out of the merry-go-round. Once out I let him conduct the little gray hackle on a subterranean tour and then — and then — I saw and heard his companion resume his greedy rise, "Slp, slp." *That* nearly unstrung me; as though one's fishing companion had yawned and casually opened and drunk a bottle of beer while one was sinking for the third time.

Like a harried dime-store manager with the place full of reaching juvenile delinquents, I kept trying to tend to business and avoid trouble and watch the sawing leader and the other feeding trout all at the same time. Then my trout began to sulk and bore, way deep, and the taut leader began to vibrate and whine like the plucked string of a harp. What if he snags a deadhead? I fretted. Just then a whirring half-dozen local ducks rushed upstream in oiled flight, banking away when they saw this strange tableau, a queer man standing there holding a straining hoop. Finally worried, I tried a little more pressure, gently pumping, and he came up in a sudden rush and rolled on his side at my feet like a length of cordwood. Then he saw his tormentor and was down and away again.

The nighthawks had descended to join the bats before I had him folded and dripping in the net, stone dead. "Holy old Mackinaw!" I said, numb-wristed and weak with conquest. A noisy whippoorwill announced dusk. I blew on my matted gray hackle and, without changing flies, on the next business cast I was on to his partner — the senior partner, it developed — which I played far into the night, the nighthawks and bats wheeling all about me. Two days later all three of us appeared in the local paper; on the front page, mind you. I was the one in the middle, the short one with the fatuous grin.

Next season I rather think I'll visit my secret place once or twice.

BYME-BY-TARPON

To capture the fish is not all of the fishing. Yet there are circumstances which make this philosophy hard to accept. I have in mind an incident of angling tribulation which  rivals the most poignant instant of my boyhood, when a great trout flopped for one sharp moment on a mossy stone and then was gone like a golden flash into the depths of the pool.

Some years ago I followed Attalano, my guide, down the narrow Mexican street of Tampico to the bank of the broad Panuco. Under the rosy dawn the river quivered like a restless opal. The air, sweet with the song of blackbird and meadowlark, was full of cheer; the rising sun shone in splendor on the water and the long line of graceful palms lining the opposite bank, and the tropical forest beyond, with its luxuriant foliage festooned by gray moss. Here was a day to warm the heart of any fisherman; here was the beautiful river, celebrated in many a story; here was the famous guide, skilled with oar and gaff, rich in experience. What sport I would have; what treasure of keen sensation would I store; what flavor of life would I taste this day! Hope burns always in the heart of the fisherman.

Attalano was in harmony with the day and the scene. He had a cheering figure, lithe and

ZANE GREY

erect, with a springy stride, bespeaking the Montezuma blood said to flow in his Indian veins. Clad in a colored cotton shirt, blue jeans, and Spanish girdle, and treading the path with brown feet never deformed by shoes, he would have stopped an artist. Soon he bent his muscular shoulders to the oars, and the ripples circling from each stroke hardly disturbed the calm Panuco. Down the stream glided long Indian canoes, hewn from trees and laden with oranges and bananas. In the stern stood a dark native wielding an enormous paddle with ease. Wild-fowl dotted the glossy expanse; white cranes and pink flamingoes graced the reedy bars; red-breasted kingfishers flew over with friendly screech. The salt breeze kissed my cheek; the sun shone with the comfortable warmth Northerners welcome in spring; from over the white sand-dunes far below came the faint boom of the ever-restless Gulf.

We trolled up the river and down, across from one rush-lined lily-padded shore to the other, for miles and miles with never a strike. But I was content, for over me had been cast the dreamy, care-dispelling languor of the South.

When the first long, low swell of the changing tide rolled in, a stronger breeze raised little dimpling waves and chased along the water in dark, quick-moving frowns. All at once the tarpon began to show, to splash, to play, to roll. It was as though they had been awakened by the stir and murmur of the miniature breakers. Broad bars of silver flashed in the sunlight, green backs cleft the little billows, wide tails slapped lazily on the water. Every yard of river seemed to hold a rolling fish. This sport increased until the long stretch of

water, which had been as calm as St. Regis Lake at twilight, resembled the quick current of a Canadian stream. It was a fascinating, wonderful sight. But it was also peculiarly exasperating, because when fish roll in this sportive, lazy way they will not bite. For an hour I trolled through this whirlpool of flying spray and twisting tarpon, with many a salty drop on my face, hearing all around me the whipping crash of breaking water.

"Byme-by-tarpon," presently remarked Attalano, favoring me with the first specimen of his English.

The rolling of the tarpon diminished, and finally ceased as noon advanced.

No more did I cast longing eyes upon those huge bars of silver. They were buried treasure. The breeze quickened as the flowing tide gathered strength, and together they drove the waves higher. Attalano rowed across the river into the outlet of one of the lagoons. This narrow stream was unruffled by wind; its current was sluggish and its muddy waters were clarifying under the influence of the now fast-rising tide.

By a sunken log near shore we rested for lunch. I found the shade of the trees on the bank rather pleasant, and became interested in a blue heron, a russet-colored duck, and a brown-and-black snipe, all sitting on the sunken log. Near by stood a tall crane watching us solemnly, and above in the treetop a parrot vociferously proclaimed his knowledge of our presence. I was wondering if he objected to our invasion, at the same time taking a most welcome bite for lunch, when directly in front of me the water flew up as if propelled by some submarine power. Framed in a shower of spray I saw an immense tarpon, with mouth agape and fins stiff, close in pursuit of frantically leaping little fish.

The fact that Attalano dropped his sandwich attested to the large size and close proximity of the tarpon. He uttered a grunt of satisfaction and pushed out the boat. A school of feeding tarpon closed the mouth of the lagoon. Thousands of mullet had been cut off from their river haunts and were now leaping, flying, darting in wild haste to elude the great white monsters. In the foamy swirls I saw streaks of blood.

"Byme-by-tarpon!" called Attalano, warningly.

Shrewd guide! I had forgotten that I held a rod. When the realization dawned on me that sooner of later I would feel the strike of one of these silver tigers a keen, tingling thrill of excitement quivered over me. The primitive man asserted himself; the instinctive lust to conquer and to kill seized me, and I leaned forward, tense and strained with suspended breath and swelling throat.

Suddenly the strike came, so tremendous in its energy that it almost pulled me from my seat; so quick, fierce, bewildering that I could think of nothing but to hold on. Then the water split with a hissing sound to let out a great tarpon, long as a door, seemingly as wide, who shot up and up into the air. He wagged his head and shook it like a struggling wolf. When he fell back with a heavy splash, a rainbow, exquisitely beautiful and delicate, stood out of the spray, glowed, paled, and faded.

Five times he sprang toward the blue sky, and as many he plunged down with a thunderous crash. The reel screamed. The line sang. The rod, which I had thought stiff as a tree, bent like a willow wand. The silver king came up far astern and sheered to the right in a long, wide curve, leaving behind a white wake. Then he sounded, while I watched the line with troubled eyes. But not long did he sulk. He began a series of magnificent tactics new in my experience. He stood on his tail, then on his head; he sailed like a bird; he shook himself so violently as to make a convulsive, shuffling sound; he dove, to come up covered with mud, marring his bright sides; he closed his huge gills with a slap and, most remarkable of all, he rose in the shape of a crescent, to straighten out with such marvelous power that he seemed to actually crack like a whip.

After this performance, which left me in a condition of mental aberration, he sounded again, to begin a persistent, dragging pull which was the most disheartening of all his maneuvers; for he took yard after yard of line until he was far away from me, out in the Panuco. We followed him, and for an hour crossed to and fro, up and down, humoring him, responding to his every caprice, as if he verily were a king. At last, with a strange inconsistency more human than fishlike, he returned to the scene of his fatal error, and here in the mouth of the smaller stream he leaped once more. But it was only a ghost of his former efforts — a slow, weary rise, showing he was tired. I could see it in the weakening wag of his head. He no longer made the line whistle.

I began to recover the long line. I pumped and reeled him closer. Reluctantly he came, not yet broken in spirit, though his strength had sped. He rolled at times with a shade of the old vigor, with a pathetic manifestation of the temper that became a hero. I could see the long, slender tip of his dorsal fin, then his broad tail and finally the gleam of his silver side. Closer he came and slowly circled around the boat, eyeing me with great, accusing eyes. I measured him with a fisherman's glance. What a great fish! Seven feet, I calculated, at the very least.

At this triumphant moment I made a horrible discovery. About six feet from the leader the strands of the line had frayed, leaving only one thread intact. My blood ran cold and the clammy sweat broke out on my brow. My empire was not won; my first tarpon was as if he had never been. But true to my fishing instincts, I held on morosely; tenderly I handled him; with brooding care I riveted my eye on the frail place in my line, and gently, ever so gently, I began to lead the silver king shoreward. Every smallest move of his tail meant disaster to me, so when he moved it I let go of the reel. Then I would have to coax him to swim back again.

The boat touched the bank. I stood up and carefully headed my fish toward the shore, and slid his head and shoulders out on the lily pads. One moment he lay there, glowing like mother-of-pearl, a rare fish, fresh from the sea. Then, as Attalano warily reached for the leader, he gave a gasp, a flop that deluged us with muddy water, and a lunge that spelled freedom.

I watched him swim slowly away with my bright leader dragging beside him. Is it not the loss of things which makes life bitter? What we have gained is ours; what is lost is gone, whether fish, or use, or love, or name, or fame.

I tried to put on a cheerful aspect for my guide. But it was too soon. Attalano, wise old fellow, understood my case. A smile, warm and living, flashed across his dark face as he spoke:

"Byme-by-tarpon."

Which defined his optimism and revived the failing spark within my breast. It was, too, in the nature of a prophecy.

Clyde: the Metamorphosis

My friend Clyde awoke one morning from uneasy dreams to find himself transformed in the night into a gigantic brown trout. It was no joke. He looked around him, hoping to  see his pleasant little one-room apartment where he had lived a hermetic life since his wife cashiered him. Its walls were papered with color photographs of rising trout and natural flies the size of grouse; each corner held three or four bamboo rods in aluminum tubes; the chests of drawers were crammed with blue-dun necks and flies and fly boxes and his thirteen Princess reels; the windowsills and bookcases were packed solid with hundreds of books and catalogs and magazines devoted to the sport to which he had devoted his life. They were not there. Neither were his hands, which were fins.

Instead, he was suspended in cold moving water under an old upturned maple stump. From the clarity and size of the water, he deduced he was in Montana, or perhaps Idaho. That was fine with Clyde. If he was going to be a trout, and he had often meditated on what it would be like to be a trout (so he could tell how they thought), he'd just as well be one in Montana and Idaho.

"Well, this love of fly fishing sure takes me places I otherwise wouldn't go," he thought.

NICK LYONS

And as soon as he thought this, he realized, since he was thinking, that he had resolved an age-old problem. If he, existing under that old tree stump, could think, he could analyze his own thoughts; and since what was true for him would have to be true for all trout, he could learn what any trout thought. He was glad he had read Descartes and Kant before he went on the Halford binge.

Curiously, his esoteric studies had led him closer and closer to this point. Only the night before he had been sitting in the dimly lit room, sunk deep into his armchair in front of the lit fish-tank in which swam Oscar, his pet brown. He had been staring intently, reciting a mantra, meditating, as he did every night for four hours, when, for a moment — no, it could not be true — Oscar had (at least he thought so) told him that Foolex dubbing was the ultimate solution to the body problem. "Not quill ribbing?" he had asked audibly. "Definitely not," said Oscar. "I like you so I'll give you the straight poop: Foolex is where it's at. Anyway, tomorrow it . . . oh, you'll find out."

And so he had.

He had a thousand questions and worked his way a bit upstream, where he saw a pretty spotted tail waving gently back and forth. The trout, a hen, about three pounds, shifted slightly as Clyde nudged her and eyed him suspiciously: it was still three weeks before spawning season and she was feeling none too frisky. He opened his mouth to ask her about Foolex bodies and careened back in the current. The henfish, named Trudy, thought he was a dumb cluck and that she ought to work her way quickly past the riffle

into the upper pool. Maybe this bird's clock was wrong; though she had a rotten headache, he might even attack her.

Clyde, ever watchful, immediately deduced from her defensiveness that communication among trout, like communication between fly fishermen and bocce players, was impossible. He'd have to answer his questions by himself. This is never easy, particularly not on an empty stomach. He had not eaten anything since the pepperoni sandwich fifteen hours earlier; and he was not dumb enough to think he could soon get another, since the Belle Deli was two thousand miles away.

There was a silver flash and Clyde turned and shot up after it, turning on it as it slowed and turned and lifted up in the current. But he was too late. A little twelve-inch rainbow had sped from behind a large rock and grasped the thing, and it was now struggling with ludicrous futility across stream, the silver object stuck in its lower jaw.

"Incredible!" Clyde thought. "How could I have been so dumb?" He had not seen the hooks; he had not distinguished between metal and true scales. If he who had studied Halford, Skues, Marinaro, and Schwiebert could not distinguish a C. P. Swing from a dace tartare, what hope had any of his speckled kin? He shivered with fear as he asked himself: "Are *all* trout this dumb?"

He worked his way back under the upturned stump, into the eddy, and sulked. This was a grim business. He noticed he was trembling with acute anxiety neurosis but could not yet accept that *all* trout were neurotic. He was positively starved now and would

34

have risen to spinach, which he hated.

Bits and pieces of debris, empty nymph shucks, a couple of grubs swept into the eddy. He nosed them, bumped them, took them into his mouth, spit some of them out. By noon he had managed to nudge loose one half-dead stone-fly nymph, *Pteronarcys californica*; he had nabbed one measly earthworm; and he had found a few cased caddises. Most food, he noted, came off the bottom; that's where it was at. The lure had come down from the surface; he should have known. He was learning something new every minute.

By now he had recognized that he was in the Big Hole River, below Divide; he was sure he had once fished the pool. Settled into that eddy under the stump, he now knew why he had not raised a fish here: the current swung the food down below the undercut bank, but his flies had been too high up in the water. The way to fish this run was almost directly downstream from his present position, casting parallel to the bank so the nymph would have a chance to ride low and slip down into the eddy.

He was trying to plot the physics of the thing, from below, and was getting dizzy, when he realized he could starve flat down to death if he didn't stop trying to be a trout fisherman and settle for being a trout. His stomach felt pinched and dry; his jaws ached to clamp down on a fresh stone-fly nymph or, yes, a grasshopper. That's what he wanted. He suddenly had a mad letch for grasshoppers — and there was absolutely nothing he could do to get one. He was totally dependent on chance. "A trout's lot," he thought, "is not a happy one."

Just then the surface rippled a bit, perhaps from a breeze, and a couple of yards upstream, he saw the telltale yellow body, kicking legs, and molded head of a grasshopper. It was August, and he knew the grasshoppers grew large around the Big Hole at that time of the year. It came at him quickly, he rose sharply to it, then stopped and turned away with a smirk. "Not me. Uh-uh. A Dave's Hopper if I ever saw one. Not for this guy." And as he thought this, Trudy swept downstream past him, too quick for him to warn, and nabbed the thing in an abrupt little splash. Then she turned, swam up by him, seemed to shake her head and say, "How dumb a cluck can you be?"

So it *had* been the real thing. Nature was imitating art now. Oh, he could taste the succulent hopper.

Another splatted down, juicy and alive, and he rose again, paused, and it shot downstream in a rush. He'd never know about that one.

Oh, the existential torment of it! "And I thought deciding which artificial fly to use was hard!"

Two more hoppers, then a third splatted down. He passed up one, lost a fin-race with Trudy for the third. She was becoming a pill.

He could bear it no longer. He'd even eat a Nick's Crazylegs if it came down. Anything. Anything to be done with the torment, the veil of unknowing, the inscrutability, which was worse than the pain in his gut, as it always is.

And then he saw it.

It was a huge, preposterous, feathered thing with a big black hook curled up under it. Some joker with three thumbs had thought it looked like a grasshopper. The body was made of Foolex. How could Oscar possibly have thought that body anything other than insulting? Clyde's hook jaw turned up in a wry smile; he wiggled his adipose fin. The fly came down over him and he watched it safely from his eddy. And it came down again. Then again. Twelve. Thirteen times. Trudy had moved twice in its direction. He could tell she was getting fairly neurotic about it.

Foolex? That body could not fool an imbecile. It *was* an insult!

Eighteen. Twenty times the monstrosity came over him. He was fuming now. How *dare* someone throw something like that at him! Had they no respect whatsoever? If that's all fishermen thought of him, what did it matter. He was bored and hungry and suffering from a severe case of *angst* and humiliation. Nothing mattered. It was a trout's life.

He rose quickly and surely now, turning as the thing swept past him on the thirty-third cast. He saw it hang in the surface eddy for a moment. He opened his mouth. Foolex? It infuriated him! It was the ultimate insult.

He lunged forward. And at the precise moment he knew exactly what trout see and why they strike, he stopped being a trout.

38

SKELTON'S PARTY

"Ma'am, you want to hand me that lunch so I can stow it?" Skelton took the wicker basket from Mrs. Rudleigh; and then the Thermos she handed him. "I've got plenty of water," he said.

"That's not water."

"What is it?"

"Gibsons."

"Let me put that in the cooler for you then — "

"We put them in the Thermos," said Rudleigh, "so we don't have to put them in the cooler. We like them where we can get at them. In case we need them, you know, real snappy."

Tom Skelton looked up at him. Most people when they smile expose a section of their upper teeth; when Rudleigh smiled, he exposed his lower teeth.

"Hold the Thermos in your lap," Skelton said. "If that starts rolling around the skiff while I'm running these banks, I'll throw it overboard."

"An ecologist," said Mrs. Rudleigh.

"Are you sure Nichol cannot appeal his sentence, Captain?" said Rudleigh.

"I'm sure," said Skelton.

Mrs. Rudleigh reached out one hand and bent it backward so her fingernails were all in

THOMAS MCGUANE

display; she was thinking of a killer line but it wouldn't come; so she didn't speak.

Skelton knew from other guides he could not let the clients run the boat for him; but he had never expected this; now all three of them were glancing past one another with metallic eyes.

Mrs. Rudleigh came and Skelton put her in the forward chair. Rudleigh followed in squeaking bright deck shoes and sat aft, swiveling about in the chair with an executive's preoccupation.

"Captain," Rudleigh began. Men like Rudleigh believed in giving credit to the qualified. If an eight-year-old were running the skiff, Rudleigh would call him "Captain" without irony; it was a credit to his class. "Captain, are we going to bonefish?" Mrs. Rudleigh was putting zinc oxide on her thin nose and on the actual edges of her precise cheekbones. She was a thin, pretty woman of forty who you could see had a proclivity for hysterics, slow burns, and slapping.

"We have a good tide for bonefish."

"Well, Missus Rudleigh and I have had a good deal of bonefishing in Yucatán and we were wondering if it mightn't be an awfully long shot to fish for permit..."

Skelton knew it was being put to him; finding permit — big pompano — was a guide's hallmark and he didn't particularly have a permit tide. "I can find permit," he said though, finishing a sequence Rudleigh started with the word "Captain."

Carter strolled up. He knew the Rudleighs and they greeted each other. "You're in

good hands," he said to them, tilting his head toward Skelton. "Boy's a regular fish hawk." He returned his head to the perpendicular.

"Where are your people, Cart?" Skelton asked to change the subject.

"They been partying, I guess. Man said he'd be late. Shortens my day."

Skelton choked the engine and started it. He let it idle for a few minutes and then freed up his lines. The canal leading away from the dock wandered around lazily, a lead-green gloss like pavement.

"Ought to find some bonefish in the Snipes on this incoming water," Carter said. Skelton looked at him a moment.

"We're permit fishing, Cart."

"Oh, really. Why, permit huh."

"What do you think? Boca Chica beach?"

"Your guess is as good as mine. But yeah okay, Boca Chica."

Skelton idled on the green tidal gloss of the canal until he cleared the entrance, then ran it up to 5,000 RPM and slacked off to an easy plane in the light chop. He leaned back over his shoulder to talk to Rudleigh. "We're going to Boca Chica beach. I think it's our best bet for permit on this tide."

"Fine, fine."

"I hate to take you there, a little bit, because it's in the landing pattern."

"I don't mind if the fish don't mind."

Skelton swung in around by Cow Key channel, past the navy hospital, under the bridge where boys were getting in some snapper fishing before it would be time for the military hospitals; then out the channel along the mangroves with the great white wing of the drive-in theater to their left, with an unattended meadow of loudspeaker stanchions; and abruptly around the corner to an expanse of blue Atlantic. Skelton ran tight to the beach, inside the boat-wrecking niggerheads; he watched for sunken ice cans and made the run to Boca Chica, stopping short.

The day was clear and bright except for one squall to the west, black with etched rain lines connecting it to sea; the great reciprocating engine of earth, thought Skelton, looks like a jellyfish.

"Go ahead and get ready, Mr. Rudleigh, I'm going to pole us along the rocky edge and see what we can see." Skelton pulled the pushpole out of its chocks and got up in the bow; Rudleigh was ready in the stern behind the tilted engine. It took two or three leaning thrusts to get the skiff under way; and then they were gliding over the sand, coral, sea fans, staghorn, and lawns of turtle grass. Small cowfish, sprats, and fry of one description or another scattered before them and vanished in the glare. Stone crabs backed away in bellicose, Pentagonian idiocy in the face of the boat's progress. Skelton held the boat into the tide at the breaking edge of the flat and looked for moving fish.

A few small sharks came early on the flood and passed down light, yellow-eyed and sweeping back and forth schematically for something in trouble. The first military

43

aircraft came in overhead, terrifyingly low; a great delta-winged machine with howling, vulvate exhausts and nervous quick-moving control flaps; so close were they that the bright hydraulic shafts behind the flaps glittered; small rockets were laid up thickly under the wings like insect eggs. The plane approached, banked subtly, and the pilot glanced out at the skiff; his head looking no larger than a cocktail onion. A moment after the plane passed, its shock wave swept toward them and the crystal, perfect world of the flat paled and vanished; not reappearing until some minutes later and slowly. The draconic roar of the engines diminished and twin blossoms of flame shrank away toward the airfield.

"It must take a smart cookie," said Mrs. Rudleigh, "to make one of those do what it is supposed to."

"It takes balls for brains," said Rudleigh.

"That's even better," she smiled.

"Only that's what any mule has," Rudleigh added.

Mrs. Rudleigh threw something at her husband, who remained in the stern, rigid as a gun carriage.

Skelton was so determined that this first day of his professional guiding be a success that he felt with some agony the ugliness of the aircraft that came in now at shorter and shorter intervals, thundering with their volatile mists drifting over the sea meadow.

The Rudleighs had opened the Thermos and were consuming its contents exactly as the heat of the day began to spread. Skelton was now poling down light, flushing small fish; then two schools of bonefish, not tailing but pushing wakes in their hurry; Rudleigh saw them late and bungled the cast, looking significantly at Mrs. Rudleigh after each failure.

"You've got to bear down," she said.

"I'm bearing down."

"Bear down harder, honey."

"I said: I'm bearing down."

Now the wading birds that were on the flat in the early tide were flooded out and flew northwest to catch the Gulf of Mexico tide. Skelton knew they had about lost their water.

"It's kind of slow, Captain," said Rudleigh.

"I've been thinking the same thing," Skelton said, his heart chilling within him. "I'm going to pole this out and make a move."

A minute later, he was running to Saddlebunch and got there in time to catch the incoming water across the big sand spot; he hardly had a moment to stake the skiff when the bonefish started crossing the sand. Now Mrs. Rudleigh was casting, driving the fish away. Rudleigh snatched the rod from her after her second failure.

"*Sit down!*"

Rudleigh was rigidly prepared for the next fish. Skelton would have helped him but knew in advance it would make things worse. He felt all of his efforts pitted against the contents of the Thermos.

"You hawse's oss," said Mrs. Rudleigh to her husband. He seemed not to have heard. He was in the vague crouch of lumbar distress.

"I can fish circles around you, queen bee," he said after a bit. "Always could."

"What about Peru? What about Cabo Blanco?"

"You're always throwing Cabo Blanco in my face without ever, repeat, ever a word about Tierra del Fuego."

"What about Piñas Bay, Panama."

"Shut up."

"Seems to me," she said, "that Raúl commented that the señora had a way of making the señor look real bum."

A small single bonefish passed the skiff. Rudleigh flushed it by casting right into its face. *"Cocksucker."*

"That's just the way you handled striped marlin. Right there is about what you did with those stripes at Rancho Buena Vista."

Rudleigh whirled around and held the point of his rod under Mrs. Rudleigh's throat. *"I'm warning you."*

"He had a tantrum at the Pez Maya Club in Yucatán," Mrs. Rudleigh told Skelton.

"Yes, ma'am. I see."

"Uh, Captain — "

"I'm right here, Mr. Rudleigh."

"I thought this was a permit deal."

"I'm looking for permit on this tide. I told you they were a long shot."

"Captain, I know about permit. I have seen permit in the Bahamas, Yucatán, Costa Rica, and at the great Belize camps in British Honduras. I know they are a long shot."

Skelton said, "Maybe your terrific familiarity with places to fish will tell us where we ought to be right now."

"Captain, I wouldn't presume."

A skiff was running just off the reel, making sheets of bright water against the sun.

"Do you know what today's tides are?" Skelton asked.

"No."

"Which way is the Gulf of Mexico?"

Rudleigh pointed all wrong. Skelton wanted to be home reading Proudhon, studying the winos, or copulating.

"Is that a permit?" Mrs. Rudleigh asked. The black fork of a large permit surfaced just out of casting range: beyond belief. Rudleigh stampeded back into position. Skelton slipped the pole out of the sand and began to ghost quietly toward the fish and stopped. Nothing visible. A long moment passed. Again, the black fork appeared.

"Cast."

Rudleigh threw forty feet beyond the permit. There was no hope of retrieving and casting again. Then out of totally undeserved luck, the fish began to change course toward Rudleigh's bait. Rudleigh and Mrs. Rudleigh exchanged glances.

"Please keep your eye on the fish." Skelton was overwhelmed by the entirely undeserved nature of what was transpiring. In a moment, the big fish was tailing again.

"Strike him."

Rudleigh lifted the rod and the fish was on. Skelton poled hard, following the fish, now streaking against the drag for deep water. The same skiff that passed earlier appeared, running the other direction; and Skelton wondered who it could be.

"God, Captain, will I be able to cope with this at all? I mean, I knew the fish was strong! But honest to God, this is a nigger with a hotfoot!"

"I'm still admiring your cast, darling."

Skelton followed watching the drawn bow the rod had become, the line shearing water with precision.

"What a marvelously smooth drag this reel has! A hundred smackers seemed steep at the time; but when you're in the breach, as I am now, a drag like this is the last nickel bargain in America!"

Skelton was poling after the fish with precisely everything he had. And it was difficult on the packed bottom with the pole inclining to slip out from under him.

His feeling of hope for a successful first-day guiding was considerably modified by

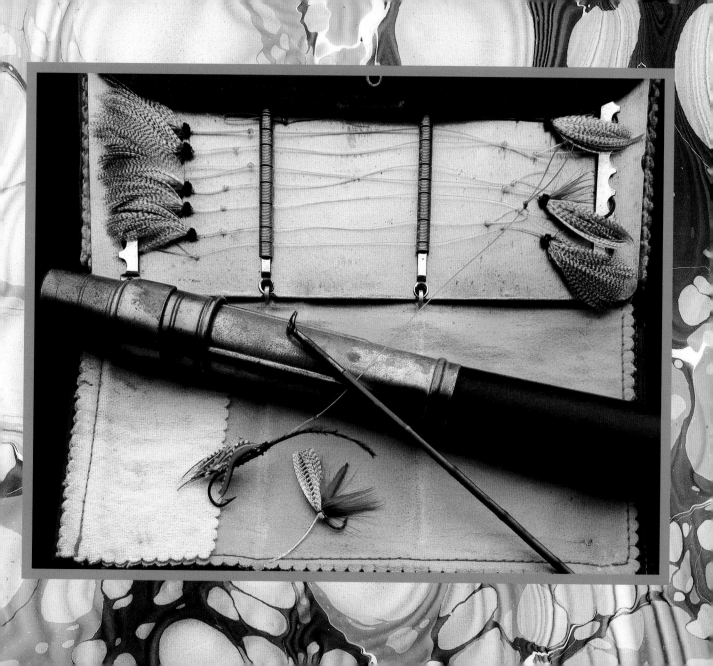

Rudleigh's largely undeserved hooking of the fish. And now the nobility of the fish's fight was further eroding Skelton's pleasure.

When they crossed the edge of the flat, the permit raced down the reef line in sharp powerful curves, dragging the line across the coral. "Gawd, gawd, gawd," Rudleigh said. "This cookie is stronger than I am!" Skelton poled harder and at one point overtook the fish as it desperately rubbed the hook on the coral bottom; seeing the boat, it flushed once more in terror, making a single long howl pour from the reel. A fish that was exactly noble, thought Skelton, who began to imagine the permit coming out of a deep-water wreck by the pull of moon and tide, riding the invisible crest of the incoming water, feeding and moving by force of blood; only to run afoul of an asshole from Connecticut.

The fight continued without much change for another hour, mainly outside the reef line in the green water over a sand bottom: a safe place to fight the fish. Rudleigh had soaked through his khaki safari clothes; and from time to time Mrs. Rudleigh advised him to "bear down." When Mrs. Rudleigh told him this, he would turn to look at her, his neck muscles standing out like cords and his eyes acquiring broad white perimeters. Skelton ached from pursuing the fish with the pole; he might have started the engine outside the reef line, but he feared Rudleigh getting his line in the propeller and he had found that a large fish was held away from the boat by the sound of a running engine.

As soon as the fish began to show signs of tiring, Skelton asked Mrs. Rudleigh to take a seat; then he brought the big net up on the deck beside him. He hoped he would be able

to get Rudleigh to release this hugely undeserved fish, not only because it was undeserved but because the fish had fought so very bravely. No, he admitted to himself,
Rudleigh would never let the fish go.

By now the fish should have been on its side. It began another long and accelerating
run, the pale sheet of water traveling higher up the line, the fish swerving somewhat
inshore again; and to his terror, Skelton found himself poling after the fish through the
shallows, now and then leaning over to free the line from a sea fan. They glided among
the little hammocks and mangrove keys of Saddlebunch in increasing vegetated conges-
tion, in a narrowing tidal creek that closed around and over them with guano-covered
mangroves and finally prevented the boat from following another foot. Nevertheless,
line continued to pour off the reel.

"Captain, consider it absolutely necessary that I kill the fish. This one doubles the
Honduran average."

Skelton did not reply, he watched the line slow its passage from the reel, winding out
into the shadowy creek; then stop. He knew there was a good chance the desperate ani-
mal had reached a dead end.

"Stay here."

Skelton climbed out of the boat and, running the line through his fingers lightly, began
to wade the tidal creek. The mosquitoes found him quickly and held in a pale globe
around his head. He waded steadily, flushing herons out of the mangroves over his head.

At one point, he passed a tiny side channel, blocking the exit of a heron that raised its stiff wings very slightly away from its body and glared at him. In the green shadows, the heron was a radiant, perfect white.

He stopped a moment to look at the bird. All he could hear was the slow musical passage of tide in the mangrove roots and the low pattern of bird sounds more liquid than the sea itself in these shallows. He moved away from the side channel, still following the line. Occasionally, he felt some small movement of life in it; but he was certain now the permit could go no farther. He had another thirty yards to go, if he had guessed right looking at Rudleigh's partially emptied spool.

Wading along, he felt he was descending into the permit's world; in knee-deep water, the small mangrove snappers, angelfish, and baby barracudas scattered before him, precise, contained creatures of perfect mobility. The brilliant blue sky was reduced to a narrow ragged band quite high overhead now and the light wavered more with the color of the sea and of estuarine shadow than that of vulgar sky. Skelton stopped and his eye followed the line back in the direction he had come. The Rudleighs were at its other end, infinitely far away.

Skelton was trying to keep his mind on the job he had set out to do. The problem was, he told himself, to go from Point A to Point B; but every breath of humid air, half sea, and the steady tidal drain through root and elliptical shadow in his ears and eyes diffused his attention. Each heron that leaped like an arrow out of his narrow slot, spiraling invisibly into the sky, separated him from the job. Shafts of light in the side channels illuminated columns of pristine, dancing insects.

Very close now. He released the line so that if his appearance at the dead end terrified the permit there would not be sufficient tension for the line to break. The sides of the mangrove slot began to yield. Skelton stopped.

An embowered, crystalline tidal pool: the fish lay exhausted in its still water, lolling slightly and unable to right itself. It cast a delicate circular shadow on the sand bottom. Skelton moved in and the permit made no effort to rescue itself; instead, it lay nearly on its side and watched Skelton approach with a steady, following eye that was, for Skelton, the last straw. Over its broad, virginal sides a lambent, moony light shimmered. The fish seemed like an oval section of sky — yet sentient and alert, intelligent as tide.

He took the permit firmly by the base of its tail and turned it gently upright in the water. He reached into its mouth and removed the hook from the cartilaginous operculum. He noticed that the suddenly loosened line was not retrieved: Rudleigh hadn't even the sense to keep tension on the line.

By holding one hand under the permit's pectoral fins and the other around the base of its tail, Skelton was able to move the fish back and forth in the water to revive it. When he first tentatively released it, it teetered over on its side, its wandering eye still fixed upon him. He righted the fish again and continued to move it gently back and forth in the water; and this time when he released the permit it stayed upright, steadying itself in equipoise, mirror sides once again purely reflecting the bottom. Skelton watched a long while until some regularity returned to the movement of its gills.

Then he cautiously — for fear of startling the fish — backed once more into the green tidal slot and turned to head for the skiff. Rudleigh had lost his permit.

The line was lying limp on the bottom. Why didn't the fool at least retrieve it? With his irritation, Skelton began to return to normal. He trudged along the creek, this time against the tide; and returned to the skiff.

The skiff was empty.

54

FISHING PRESIDENTS AND CANDIDATES

There are a dozen justifications for fishing. Among them is its importance to the political world. No political aspirant can qualify for election unless he demonstrates he is a fisherman, there being twenty-five million persons who pay annually for a license to fish.

In Roman times the people formed their political auguries by observing the flights of birds and the entrails of dead sheep. I have recently been fishing. In the long time between bites I have come to the firm conclusion that today fish take the place of the flight of birds and the entrails of sheep.

Also, I should inform you that from an augury point of view, there are two kinds of fish: there are the host of species of common or garden fish, which are the recreation of the common man. There are also the rare species of fish sought by the aristocracy of fishermen. They require more equipment and more incantations than merely spitting on the bait. Politically speaking, these fish can be ignored since they are only landed the hard way and have no appeal to most voters.

A few years ago a press photograph showed my friend, the late Senator Taft, awkwardly holding a common fish. It was taken from many angles for all the common men to

HERBERT HOOVER

see. I knew without other evidence that he was a candidate. Some years ago my friend, General Eisenhower, burst into photographs from all angles, gingerly holding three common fish. The augury was positive.

The political potency of fish is known to presidents as well as candidates. In modern times all presidents quickly begin to fish soon after election. I am told that McKinley, Taft, Wilson, and Harding all undertook fishing in a tentative way, but for the common fishes.

President Coolidge apparently had not fished before election. Being a fundamentalist in religion, economics, and fishing, he began his fish career for common trout with worms. Ten million fly-fishermen at once evidenced disturbed minds. Then Mr. Coolidge took to a fly. He gave the Secret Service guards great excitement in dodging his backcast and rescuing flies from trees. There were many photographs. Soon after that he declared he did not choose to run again.

President Franklin Roosevelt caught many common fish from the military base of a battleship.

President Truman, prior to his 1948 election, appeared once in a photograph somewhere in a boat gingerly holding a common fish in his arms. An unkind reporter wrote that someone else had caught it. I can find no trace of the letter that the reporter must have received. It is also reported that Mr. Truman was fishing somewhere north of Key West when his boat was surrounded by sharks. But sharks are always a bad augury. Mr. Truman did not run for a third term.

President Theodore Roosevelt, President Cleveland and myself — with a slight egotism! — I think, are the only presidents who had been lifelong fly-fishermen before they went to the White House.

Everyone knows of the first Roosevelt that he was a valiant hunter of big animals, and generally an evangel of the strenuous life — which included fishing. He relates an adventure with an Adirondack stream when he was twelve years old:

After dinner all of us began to "whip" the rapids. At first I sat on a rock by the water but the black flies drove me from there, so I attempted to cross the rapids. But I had miscalculated my strength for before I was half way across the force of the current had swept me into water which was above my head. Leaving the pole to take [care] of itself I struck out for a rock. My pole soon struck and so I recovered it. I then went half wading, half swimming down stream, fishing all the time but unsuccessful.

President Cleveland is author of a delightful little volume called *Fishing and Hunting Sketches*, in which he sets forth his ideas on the beatitudes of those sports. As a fisherman, he preferred small-mouthed black bass to trout, and in this respect claimed kinship to another political fisherman, Daniel Webster, from whose history he draws this interesting example of the interrelation of fishing and politics:

Perhaps [writes President Cleveland], none of Mr. Webster's orations were more notable or added more to his lasting fame than that delivered at the laying of the cornerstone of the Bunker Hill monument, and it will probably be conceded that its most impressive and beautiful passage was addressed to the survivors of the War for Independence then present, beginning with the words "Venerable Men."

This thrilling oratorical flight was composed and elaborated by Mr. Webster while wading waist deep and casting his flies in Mashapee waters. He himself afterwards often referred to this circumstance; and one who was his companion on this particular occasion has recorded the fact that, noticing indications of laxity in fishing action on Mr. Webster's part, he approached him, and that, in the exact words of this witness, "he seemed to be gazing at the overhanging trees, and presently, advancing one foot and extending his right hand, he commenced to speak — Venerable Men ...

Mr. Cleveland says that he got this story from Webster's guide, who told him that the Massachusetts Senator frequently prepared his orations in this wise, and was in the habit of addressing "mighty strong and fine talk to the fish." President Cleveland adds:

It is impossible to avoid the conclusion that the fishing habit, by promoting close association with nature, by teaching patience and by generating or stimulating useful contemplation, tends directly to the increase of the intellectual power of its votaries and through them to the improvement of our national character.

That presidents have taken to fishing in an astonishing fashion seems to me worthy of investigation. I think I have discovered the reason: it is the silent sport. One of the few opportunities given a president for the refreshment of his soul and the clarification of his thoughts by solitude lies through fishing. As I have said in another place, it is generally realized and accepted that prayer is the most personal of all human relationships. Everyone knows that on such occasions men and women are entitled to be alone and undisturbed.

Next to prayer, fishing is the most personal relationship of man; and of more importance, everyone concedes that the fish will not bite in the presence of the public, including newspapermen.

Fishing seems to be one of the few avenues left to the presidents through which they may escape to their own thoughts, may live in their own imaginings, find relief from the pneumatic hammer of constant personal contacts, and refreshment of mind in rippling waters. Moreover, it is a constant reminder of the democracy of life, of humility and of human frailty. It is desirable that the president of the United States should be periodically reminded of this fundamental fact — that the forces of nature discriminate for no man.

THE BEST RAINBOW TROUT FISHING

Rainbow trout fishing is as different from brook fishing as prizefighting is from boxing. The rainbow is called *Salmo iridescens* by those mysterious people who name the fish we catch and has recently been introduced into Canadian waters. At present the best rainbow trout fishing in the world is in the rapids of the Canadian Soo.

There the rainbow have been taken as large as fourteen pounds from canoes that are guided through the rapids and halted at the pools by Ojibway and Chippewa boatmen. It is a wild and nerve-frazzling sport and the odds are in favor of the big trout who tear off thirty or forty yards of line at a rush and then will sulk at the base of a big rock and refuse to be stirred into action by the pumping of a stout fly rod aided by a fluent monologue of Ojibwayian profanity. Sometimes it takes two hours to land a really big rainbow under those circumstances.

The Soo affords great fishing. But it is a wild nightmare kind of fishing that is second only in strenuousness to angling for tuna off Catalina Island. Most of the trout, too, take a spinner and refuse a fly, and to the ninety-nine percent pure fly fisherman, there are no one hundred percenters, that is a big drawback.

ERNEST HEMINGWAY

Of course the rainbow trout of the Soo will take a fly but it is rough handling them in that tremendous volume of water on the light tackle a fly fisherman loves. It is dangerous wading in the spots that can be waded too, for a misstep will take the angler over his head in the rapids. A canoe is a necessity to fish the very best water.

Altogether it is a rough, tough, mauling game, lacking in the meditative qualities of the Izaak Walton school of angling. What would make a fitting Valhalla for the good fisherman when he dies would be a regular trout river with plenty of rainbow trout in it jumping crazy for the fly.

There is such a one not forty miles from the Soo called the — well, called the river. It is about as wide as a river should be and a little deeper than a river ought to be and to get the proper picture you want to imagine in rapid succession the following fade-ins:

A high pine-covered bluff that rises steep up out of the shadows. A short sand slope down to the river and a quick elbow turn with a little flood wood jammed in the bend and then a pool.

A pool where the moselle-colored water sweeps into a dark swirl and expanse that is blue-brown with depth and fifty feet across.

There is the setting.

The action is supplied by two figures that slog into the picture up the trail along the riverbank with loads on their backs that would tire a packhorse. These loads are pitched over the heads onto the patch of ferns by the edge of the deep pool. That is incorrect.

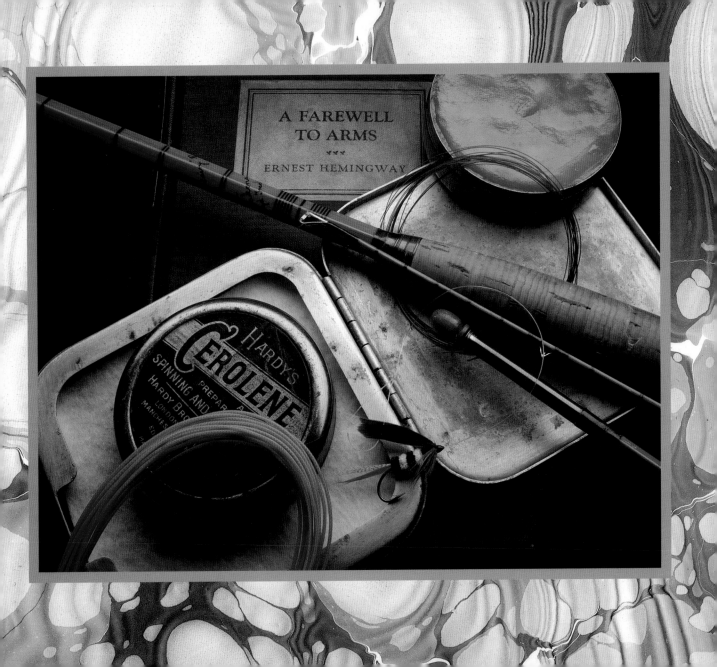

Really the figures lurch a little forward and the tump line loosens and the pack slumps onto the ground. Men don't pitch loads at the end of an eight-mile hike.

One of the figures looks up and notes the bluff is flattened on top and that there is a good place to put a tent. The other is lying on his back and looking straight up in the air. The first reaches over and picks up a grasshopper that is stiff with the fall of the evening dew and tosses him into the pool.

The hopper floats spraddle-legged on the water of the pool an instant, an eddy catches him and then there is a yard-long flash of flame, and a trout as long as your forearm has shot into the air and the hopper has disappeared.

"Did you see that?" gasped the man who had tossed in the grasshopper.

It was a useless question, for the other, who a moment before would have served as a model for a study entitled "Utter Fatigue," was jerking his fly rod out of the case and holding a leader in his mouth.

We decided on a McGinty and a Royal Coachman for the flies and at the second cast there was a swirl like the explosion of a depth bomb, the line went taut and the rainbow shot two feet out of water. He tore down the pool and the line went out until the core of the reel showed. He jumped, and each time he shot into the air we lowered the tip and prayed. Finally he jumped and the line went slack and Jacques reeled in. We thought he was gone and then he jumped right under our faces. He had shot upstream toward us so fast that it looked as though he were off.

up the Life of Wash...
...ed the quaint stor...
...was to me magic i...
...peated it. Why,...
...anted?"
...s of Rip Van...
...American boa...
...ge May 26,
...nally appea...
...ge, Charle...
produc...
...rite the...
...Following...

...Olympic The-
...Dion
with instant
...cicault
...h Theatre,
...) after which he
...enormous audiences
...from managers than ever

star.
...have charged Joseph Jefferson with
...than studying new parts and risking
...art actor—that he found it easier a...
...itable to go on playing...
...studying new plays. To this charge Jefferson
...self has made reply in characteristic fashion
cy on untried plays. The list of plays that I
...than over and over again
...self has made reply in characteristic fashion
I have often been taxed with idleness for not studying no...
...and adding them to my repertoire.
...s and of late years is certainly a very short one, and the cri...
...weary of witnessing them over and over again. Setting aside
...st their constant repetition. The list of plays that I
...st be the best judge of how to conduct
...matters connected with the course.

JOSEPH JEFFERSON (1829-1905)
AS RIP VAN WINKLE

When I finally netted him and rushed him up the bank and could feel his huge strength in the tremendous muscular jerks he made when I held him flat against the bank, it was almost dark. He measured twenty-six inches and weighed nine pounds and seven ounces.

That is rainbow trout fishing.

The rainbow takes the fly more willingly than he does bait. The McGinty, a fly that looks like a yellowjacket, is the very best. It should be tied on a number eight or ten hook.

The smaller flies get more strikes but are too small to hold the really big fish. The rainbow trout will live in the same streams with brook trout but they are found in different kinds of places. Brook trout will be forced into the shady holes under the bank and where alders hang over the banks, and the rainbow will dominate the clear pools and the fast shallows.

Magazine writers and magazine covers to the contrary, the brook, or speckled, trout does not leap out of the water after he has been hooked. Given plenty of line, he will fight a deep rushing fight. Of course if you hold the fish too tight he will be forced by the rush of the current to flop on top of the water.

But the rainbow always leaps on a slack or tight line. His leaps are not mere flops, either, but actual jumps out of and parallel with the water of from a foot to five feet. A five-foot jump by any fish sounds improbable, but it is true.

If you don't believe it, tie on to one in fast water and try and force him. Maybe if he is a five-pounder he will throw me down and only jump four feet eleven inches.

THE LINE OF LIGHT

Late the third day we went to the river. The sun looked wintry, but was still warm. Eddy was barefoot, blue-jeaned, wearing an old gray cotton pullover she'd found in my  closet. I kept gaping at that pullover: I'd fished in it for years, wiped blood and slime on it, sweated in it, smelled in it — and Eddy wore it now like Ocean wore her cloud daughters.... But I was no bloody Sun. Pullovers aside, I was miserable. I was carrying the split-cane pole and belly reel; I was stifling in waders, winter coat and fishing vest; and I was sick at heart. When we reached the river I leaned the pole against a boulder and would have taken off the coat, but Eddy put her arms around me, stood on my boots to keep her feet warm, assaulted my glum face with kisses and thanked and thanked me for cooperating with her plan.

This "plan" was the problem. It had sprung into existence an hour before, in the loft, when she told me she had to return to Portland, *alone*, by nightfall. I said nothing, but evidently it changed my appearance when my heart slithered out my mouth, rolled off the bed and landed with a squishy splat on the floor. She hugged me, said she was sorry, said not to worry, said to be happy, said Wait!

DAVID JAMES DUNCAN

Listen! she had this plan! So I listened. Part of the plan — the crucial part — was her promise to come back the very next evening. The next-best part was that when she did come back she could probably stay a solid week — "to fish the chinook run" (she winked), "at least that's what my father is going to hear." Then came the last part of the plan — the curve Mohammed the Prophet warned about: for the next two hours (after which she had to leave) I must do everything she asked me to do, provided it was "within reason, and within your power." Of course this sounded *outrageously* suspicious, but I agreed to it for two reasons: the first was that I was prepared to do anything, however chivalric, illegal or inane, to ensure the first two parts of the plan; the second was that as she proposed it she was straddling my belly, and she was naked as the sky. Who was I to argue?

The plan commenced: she had me put on warm fishing clothes, waders, winter coat and fishing vest; she asked for the shower, a towel, shampoo (she settled for Ivory soap) and the old cotton pullover; she had me fill my pockets with bread, fruit, cheese and nuts; she had me help her take things to the bus, then help her jump-start it. She dried her hair in the sun while the battery charged, shut off the engine, took my hand and said, "Now for the fun part." And she led me down to the river,

which brings us back to my glum face, to Eddy's bare feet on my boot tops, to Eddy's bare Eddy in my pullover, and to bare sunlight in Eddy's Ivory-soap-tousled hair. She turned to a river still green from the week's rain. Now and then a salmon sounded. She

squinted at the sun and the horizon. She said, "The sooner I leave the sooner I'm back. Let's get on with it."

"On with what?"

She nodded toward the river. "The fun part."

I thought the hug was the fun part, but didn't argue. She said, "What's the lightest leader you've got?"

"Three-pound."

"Tie on a three-pound leader. Use a blood-knot. Tie on a #4 hook. Give me the pole." She grinned. "God this is fun!"

I didn't agree, but did as she said, tying the rainbow lamb's wool round her waist, handing her the pole. She stepped down to the fishiest part of H2O's drift, took a deep breath and a long look at the lay of the water, then laid out an arcing cast that would have carried itself into the alders overhanging the far shore, but she braked it at the last instant and the bait fell with almost no splash into a deep slot.

"Would it damage the Plan if I asked what you're doing, Eddy?"

"I'm fishing," she said. And she was. Was she ever. She stood on a driftwood log, her toes sunk in new green moss; the red sun bathed her and her back was arced in the same sloping curve as the curve of the line sweeping down the current. I no longer recognized my old lifelong pastime: Eddy transformed it into a kind of sacred dance. And it was inconceivable to me that there could be a fish within range of her hook — be it baited or bare — that would refuse to sacrifice itself for the sake of that dance.

But there was one thing I didn't understand. I said, "There are chinooks in this drift now, Eddy, and not much else."

"I know."

"Some of them weigh fifty pounds."

"I know."

"But you're using three-pound leader."

"I know."

She stripped her line after the first cast tailed out. I said, "Even if it was possible to hook a chinook without breaking that leader, you couldn't land it if you played it all night."

"I know."

"But you said you had to leave by dark."

"I do," she said. "But *you* don't, Gus. You have to carry out the Plan!" Looking pointedly at my warm clothes, food-filled pockets and waders, she smiled the trick-or-treat smile ...

... and a bright salmon boiled in the slot.

She shot me another grin, then sent out another arcing cast: it landed perhaps forty feet upstream from where the salmon had shown. And this time Eddy stood on tiptoe, her body taut as a drawn bow, her eyes alight with water-shattered sun. My native intelligence didn't just whisper: it shouted; it sang. It said not only that the strike was inevitable, but that the fish, the river, the-trees, rocks, light and sky — all of it was made, in accordance with Immutable Laws, for beings such as Eddy, and for moments such as this.

And the line stopped drifting. The rod twitched. She lowered the tip almost to the water, letting the fish take, then she swept it back with a quick but gentle motion: the pole plunged downward. The sacred dance began.

She let line fly from the basket, applying no pressure. She whispered, "Chinook!" And when the massive silver shape rose thrashing to the surface she cackled like an old mad sage. The salmon moved upstream slowly, inexorably; Eddy gave line freely, applying so little pressure that the pole was hardly bent. Soon after the first sounding the chinook appeared to calm, moving as though it sensed no threat. It swam to the center of the drift and held behind a boulder, immovable as the boulder itself. Eddy turned. "Come here, Gus."

I had to obey.

"Untie the belly reel and put it on — quick! If the fish wants line, give it. Don't let it go slack, but don't *fight* the fish: just keep track of it. It's working!" She cackled again. "Here . . . take the pole!"

I took it. She tied the lamb's wool around my waist. Then she kissed me. "I have to go now . . . dreefee. I'll be back tomorrow, sunset. My last wish is this: *play the chinook!*" She turned and darted away toward the cabin.

If the salmon had wanted an easy getaway, then was its chance. I watched every stone her bare feet chose, watched her every stride, watched till her faded jeans and cotton pullover and yellow hair vanished in the cedars and a lump the size of an orange rose in my throat. But the fish held: it seemed to have forgotten that it was hooked. So. There I stood by the Tamanawis, alone, at sunset, wearing a belly reel, holding a split-cane pole, linked to a leviathan by an almost invisible and strategically negligible leader, with an order: *play the chinook!* It was impossible. But it was Eddy's wish — so I tried.

❀   ❀   ❀

For some time the salmon stayed behind the boulder. I held rod and line lightly, waiting, feeling the slow tail-strokes of a massive fish. Having seen its bright sides I knew it was fresh from the ocean. And it was thick as a tree, and stronger than all the white water from here to its mountain spawning bed. With ten-pound test and a full day ahead I might have had some chance: I had three-pounds and the sun stood on the sea. But Eddy didn't say "Catch it." She said, "Play it!" She meant it to be a game. She knew I'd never land it — but to try not to lose it . . . well, it was something to do while she was away. What would I have done in the cabin but pule in the wine glass, pining for her return? And what would it be like to play a fish as long as it could be played, knowing from the start that I'd never catch it? Maybe I was just moonstruck, but I was beginning to like the idea. "All right fish," I said, "All right Gus. Take it slow. No tension in the head, or in the hands, or in the line."

I looked at my hands in the last of the light, saw the red groundwater flowing under

74

the pale skin, thought of Nick and his pierced palm, thought of the tiny flies I'd tied, thought of great or implausible things that human hands had accomplished — and the old inner glimmerings that sent me up the River Road began once again. When the chinook began to move, I was ready.

It didn't wait to test me: it rounded the boulder on the far side and the nylon line raked the rock, but I jumped up on a log, stood on tiptoe, sent the rod-tip toward the sky — and the sharper angle freed the line. The fish moved out, surging up through H2O's drift with calm, sure tail strokes. I eased my grip, slowed my breath, let the line run smoothly out between left thumb and forefinger. And as I set out after the salmon I realized what had begun: the pain of the hook forgotten, it had resumed its anadromous migration. It was journeying freely toward its spawning grounds, and because it sensed no tension in the too-light line, I, a landsman, could mark its course and follow!

It moved quickly, right up the center of the current. In the slow water at the tail of the next riffle I had to jog to keep close, but in the pool above it rested, giving me a chance to scramble over logs and catch up. The sun was gone now, but a gray light in the east promised the moonrise. The moon would be full — which meant the salmon would all be travelling — and there was a thin cover of cirrus to reflect its light, making the night almost day-bright, but blanketing it against the cutting cold of the night I'd spent on the way to the source. The chinook picked up its pace again. I payed out the line and followed. Because of the concentration it took to maintain the tensionless tension I forgot my feet, but — as often happens when fishermen follow fish — they picked their own way over the logs and rocks, unerring. The river wasn't high, and this was to my advantage: there was a wide stony shoulder to walk, clear of the stream-side brush. The fish thrust steadily up through a long array of glides and easy rapids, and I soon lost track of time. I was bent in keeping the line taut but tensionless: how long, how far, how smoothly we traveled — all was up to the fish.

When the salmon sidled toward my side of the river I had to crouch to keep from being seen. Sometimes it swam in shoals not two rod-lengths away. It entered such a shoal just as the moonbeams sank into the water and I saw it perfectly — a pulsing, silvery shape the size of a dog, hovering in an element as clear as air. The sight of it so fascinated me that I stumbled, the line tensed, the hook stung the salmon's mouth — and the shallows exploded! The chinook plunged into the mainstream with strokes like the strides of a running elk. Any hidden notions I'd had of capturing it were destroyed: the power in its thrusts was awesome. I scrambled upstream as fast as I could, but the fish surged so far ahead that the reel nearly emptied, and then the current's pull put tension in the line, driving the hook deeper. The chinook began to bulldog. I knew then that if tooth touched leader, the game was up. I gathered the lost line, caught up with the salmon, erased all the tension. The bulldogging stopped: the leader held. Eddy must have hooked it perfectly, at the very edge of the jaw.

After a long wait the fish resumed its migration at the early, regal pace. Watching the line cut the shimmering river, I followed.

* * *

The chinook moved up the Tamanawis with the ease of a cloud shadow gliding up a valley. After many pools it slid in behind another rock and held. I waited. The moon rose higher. When the fish didn't move I found a rock myself, and sat. I zipped my coat, ate cheese and an apple, even smoked a pipe. It seemed the chinook waited for me. Perhaps we were making friends. Some night bird approached down the river corridor, gliding for long, silent spaces, then thrusting its wings just once, then gliding some more: it was swimming breaststroke through the air. When it neared me it wheeled into the trees with a hooing cry and I recognized a great horned owl. As if the cry were a sign, the salmon moved out.

As time and water passed I got better at the game. The moon brightened my rocky path, and it seemed that the deeper the fish and I journeyed into the night the less cautious I had to be. Only in the shallow rapids was there frenzy to the chinook's pace; in riffle, pool, eddy and glide it proceeded with stately calm. Perhaps its wound was numb now; perhaps its ancient instincts told it that night meant safety no matter what dark shapes might follow beyond the fringe of the water; or perhaps it was aware of me all along and simply grew used to me. Whatever the reason, I walked more and more boldly, no longer crouching, no longer tiptoeing over the stones. And much more often than not the salmon seemed to choose my side of the river — as if it preferred my company. I couldn't get used to this: I know the fish could see me plainly, yet it swam at its unaltering pace along a close, parallel path. In places I had to wade to stay clear of overhanging brush or log jams, but in time even my splashing didn't cause the chinook to shy. I really think the fish grew curious, wondering who on earth was walking beside it through the night.

As my walking and wading and attending to the line became less conscious, more free and easy, I found I could free my mind. My thoughts of Eddy were constant as the sound of the river, but beneath or beside them I found myself remembering Titus, talking about the ancient Taoists — and of an "Equilibrium" of which they spoke. He said this Equilibrium derived from a kind of inner balance: it transmitted itself from the soul to the mind, and from the mind to the body, and when a man possessed of it put his hand to an art or craft he was capable of unheard-of feats. The masters of Zen archery, the Sufi poets, the Taoist landscape painters, the early Celtic mariners — these people had this Equilibrium. The Fianna of pre-Christian Ireland, the master painters of Persian miniatures, the architects of the great mosques and gothic cathedrals — they possessed it as well. And just as I'd wondered whether Thomas Bigeater might have possessed it Titus said that in China there had been simple fishermen who, because of this Equilibrium, could catch enormous fish using cane-poles and a *single strand* of silk. "A line breaks," Titus said, "at a stress point. But if the fisherman experiences no stress, and if he transmits this experience through his hands to his pole, to his line, to his hook, then there will be no stress point, therefore no

point at which the strand can break." By virtue of this principle, he said, these fishermen could hook the biggest fish that swam and still coax them at last into their waiting hands....

I tried to invoke the peace I'd felt during the long days of rain watching, to find again that empty place inside me; I sensed that if I could constantly know such a peace, if I could be filled with such an emptiness, then I might come to possess this Equilibrium....

Then I burst out laughing. The emptiness was gone — utterly gone....

Because Eddy had come: she'd come and filled it, and overflowed it, and there was no better name for what shone there now but *love. Eddy had come!* and as I walked with the salmon that love overwhelmed me, and I laughed like a drunk in the night. I thought, *Why shouldn't love be my Equilibrium?* Why shouldn't love be the forceless force running from heart to hand, down the line to the hook, from the hook through the wound and into the fish? Couldn't love create that sacred balance? Wouldn't love dissolve all stress? And from my depths came a wavelike rush of certainty: love *could* sustain the frailest of lines! As long as I loved I would not lose this salmon. It didn't matter how big or strong it was: with love alone coursing down the line it would have no desire to escape!

As the moon climbed the sky so the fish and I climbed the river, without struggle, almost without effort. I'd already sensed that the chinook had come to trust me, and soon after I saw that so, it seemed, did the animals and the birds. A second owl, breaststroking down the corridor like the first, did not wheel away but coasted over in silence, its bewildering eyes glaring as it passed over my rod-tip. In an eddying backwash a pair of raccoons hunted crawdads: they mounted a rock as I strolled past, and bossed me in soft, clicking bandito voices — but when I held out the last of the goat cheese they let me come near and place it on the rock between them. The first deer I saw were yearlings, so I took their lack of caution to be inexperience — but later a four-point blacktail buck let me near enough to roll him an apple, watched while I passed, then bent his neck to eat it. Still later a beaver paddled by and neither slapped its tail nor plunged under. And when I crossed a gravel bar where seven mergansers slept they untucked heads from wings at the sound of my feet, but neither swam nor flew as my line passed right over them. And with each of these encounters the love deepened, and the certainty grew. It had always been my way to approach the river like a wanded magician out to work deception. But this night, thanks to Eddy, thanks to love, I came as a blind man led by a seeing-eye salmon — and it showed me a world I'd believed was destroyed, a world where a man could still walk unfeared among the animals and birds he calls "wild."

Moved and shamed by the animals' trust, feeling hour after hour the faithful pulse of the salmon's tail beating like the river's silver heart, I felt the fisherman in me being unmade. The angler/fish, hunter/quarry paradigm began melting away like blood in water. There could be no question, with so light a line, of ever bringing this fish to bay. There could be no betrayal, no treachery, no struggle and death. There was only a chinook on its primordial journey, and an undone fisherman following, being led deeper into the night.

❀   ❀   ❀

The salmon's pace remained steady and untiring. My fatigue grew, my thoughts slowed, my feet would sometimes stumble. But my hands kept pulsing the heart's secret down the line, through the water, to the fish.

As I looked out of myself, unthinking, the night grew more and more extraordinary, yet more and more familiar: I felt as though I were returning to some forgotten, ancient home. The river shimmered and glowed and shattered the moon, flowing from east to west like the horizontal bar of a cross; the line, too, shone pale in the light, reaching vertically from sky to water. The cirrus cover thinned away into a high mist, and a huge and pale spherical rainbow encompassed and journeyed with the moon. The moist sky with its few faint stars seemed to flow like a boundless river, and the Tamanawis with its glittering bands of moonshine seemed like a ribbon of Milky-Wayed sky. I felt overturned and overwhelmed, and walked in a slow hush, awed by all I'd seen and was seeing, yet I sensed that still greater secrets were impending.

Now and then in the deeper pools other salmon would roll close to mine. In a glassy glide above one such pool I saw that my fish had drawn companions — an escort of scurrying jacks, darting crisscross in its wake. I knew then that my guide was a female, laden with eggs; and I knew that if by some miracle I should coax her into my grasp, I could never harm her. She swam on and on, seeming even statelier now compared to the veering, nervous jacks. In one violent rapid I know the line dragged and she felt the sting of the hook. But after so long an association it seemed not to disturb her: she swam on with the calm, sure strokes of one who knows she carries the hope of her people. She swam fearlessly, though she swam toward her death.

In a wide, leaf-strewn eddy my fish drew near me and I looked for the trailing jacks: I was thinking I watched her shadow when the dark patch suddenly eased ahead — it was another big chinook. When they continued to swim in tandem I realized she'd found her mate. The buck, too, grew used to my presence, though he was not so tolerant of splashing; I tried to keep more to the shore. But often they would come close to me, letting me watch them journey together, breathing the wind woven into the water as I breathed the ether entwined in the air. Animals and night birds called out to one another, marking our passage. The haloed moon crossed the sky. The salmon led me up the river while men were sleeping. And the newly bestirred love coursed through me as steadily and easily as the light line cut through the water.

Far, far later, in the hour before dawn, the two salmon came to rest behind a fallen tree in waist-deep water. The moon and rainbow slipped toward the sea. I knew the night journey was ending: the two chinooks would stay here till first light, then move on to the next deep pool to wait out the day. My companion hovered by her mate with such tranquility: I wanted our parting to be tranquil.

I began to wade in toward her. Both of them saw me, yet made no move. Inch by inch I crept toward them, hardly stirring the water, feeling my legs had turned to water, making no sound. When I was exactly a rod-length away I laid my pole down on the river and took the line in my hands. I waded on until the hooked salmon hovered at my knees. I was too tired for dumb amazement, but her tameness and the throb of her hovering stirred me like music heard in sleep. Moving nothing but my fingers, I drew in the line. When it came taut my fish tensed, but stayed where she was. I waited for the pink and blue bands of the moon's rainbow to sink past the tip of the tallest fir, then again I drew in line: I pulled it toward me in increments, praying that she wouldn't fear. Still she stayed. Then slowly, so slowly, I leaned down toward her;

my fingers touched the water: she saw them crease the river surface, but still she held. I bent lower — trying to enter the river with the imperceptible motion of sinking moons or suns. I kept my hands together as I inched in the line; the water numbed them, yet more than ever they pulsed with strange certainty, pulsed in obedience to secret law. My arms sank silently; my sleeves filled with water; I felt the blood-knot; I began to inch in the invisible leader. The buck grew skittish and moved away, circled, brushed against my salmon, circled again: but only she had felt the hook and watched the line all through the night. She stayed.

I drew in line till only inches separated my hand from her. I held the line with my right hand, but with my left I reached still lower. Now my hair touched the water, my beard, my face. I drew a long breath and bent still lower....

My face entered the river; I felt my ears fill; the water poured in at the neck of my coat

and ran freezing down my chest. I opened my eyes: she was blurred to me now, but still my salmon hadn't moved. I slipped my numbed left hand down. I touched her moonlit silver side —

and still she held, unmoving. I rested my cold hand upon her gleaming side. She suffered my touch, and stayed.

My breath ran out. I had to draw away. Water poured from me to the river, and still my salmon stayed. So at last, with the slightest tug, I let the line be broken at the blood knot. Bearing the hook, trailing the wisp of unseen leader, the chinook eased slowly away.

I wiped the water from my face. I lifted the pole off the face of the water. I walked toward the River Road and home.